TEST YO
ON 1
RULL OF
THE ROAD

BASIL MOSENTHAL

Adlard Coles Nautical
LONDON

CONTENTS

This book is published as a companion volume to

LEARNING THE RULE OF THE ROAD
A Guide for the Crews and Skippers of Small Craft
by Basil Mosenthal

Published by Adlard Coles Nautical
ISBN 0 7136 6150 X

INTRODUCTION

Although usually referred to as 'The Rule of the Road', the official title is *The International Regulations for Preventing Collisions at Sea* (the abbreviation 'Colregs' is also used). For brevity in this book we shall refer to them as the 'Rules'.

A good knowledge of the Rules is required for the various RYA yachtmaster exams, but this is not just a matter of acquiring theoretical knowledge; knowing the Rules well is essential for keeping out of trouble at sea.

Many of today's sailing areas are becoming increasingly congested, and often when you go afloat you may come across a 'who should give way to whom?' situation to which you must know the answer instinctively.

You might not often come across the lights of a tug with a tow, however, but when you do there will be no time to go below and consult the book; you will have to realise immediately what you are looking at, and take the appropriate action.

The Rules themselves are long and detailed because they have to cover every possible situation. An effective way to check your knowledge of the Rules is to ask yourself questions, or – if you are afloat – share them around the cockpit with the rest of the crew. If you can learn the correct answers to all the questions in this book, you can assume that you at least have a good working knowledge of the Rules.

ABOUT THE QUESTIONS

The Rule of the Road applies to all vessels whether they be supertankers or small yachts; which means that they must be known by all skippers, regardless of the size of vessel.

Nevertheless, to be realistic, the various Rules and their application will have a rather different significance for small craft than for large merchant vessels. Therefore, while the questions in this book cover all the Rules, they concentrate on aspects of particular concern to small craft.

THE QUESTIONS

The questions (always featured beneath a blue heading bar) are arranged in sections, which refer to the practical application of the Rules. Section 7, as the name suggests, is a mixed bag and contains questions taken from all parts of the Rules, dealing with some subjects that have already been covered in the earlier sections. It also contains a few questions about Distress Signals, and while these are not strictly part of the Rule of the Road, they are covered by an annex to the Rules.

THE ANSWERS

The answers to each set of questions (featured beneath a green heading bar) are found by simply turning the page. The authors have tried to explain things as fully as possible; should you wish to refresh your memory, the answers are cross-referenced to the relevant section of the Rules which are included in full at the end of the book.

SECTION 1 • GENERAL & DEFINITIONS

1. When the Rules apply to sailing vessels, what is the exact definition of a 'sailing vessel'?

2. What is the definition of being 'under way'?

3. Although it is usually obvious, how do the Rules define the 'windward' side of a vessel?

4. The Rules say that, at any time, a vessel must proceed at a safe speed, and that a safe speed must depend on the prevailing conditions. Can you name at least three of these 'prevailing conditions'?

5. Perhaps strangely, the Rules do not only require a good look-out by sight, but what else as well?

6. What specific instructions are given to a vessel that has to keep clear of another – ie the 'give way' vessel?

7. The 'stand-on' vessel is instructed to maintain her course and speed. Under what circumstances should she do otherwise?

8. When is a vessel said to be 'constrained by her draught'?

9. When is a vessel said to be 'not under command'?

10. When making sound signals, what is the definition of a 'long blast' and a 'short blast'?

11. What are the implications of a vessel showing that she is 'restricted in her ability to manoeuvre'?

1. A sailing vessel is any vessel under sail which is not using her motor to assist her progress. As soon as she turns on her motor for propulsion (not just to charge her batteries) she becomes, as far as the Rules are concerned, a power vessel. [*3(c)*]

2. A vessel 'under way' is not at anchor, made fast to the shore or aground. [*3(i)*]

3. The windward side is considered to be the opposite side to that on which the mainsail is being carried. [*12(b)*]

4. Prevailing conditions to be taken into account for safe speed are:
   - The state of visibility.
   - Traffic density including the presence of fishing vessels.
   - Manoeuverability of own vessel, including stopping distance.
   - At night, background light from shore lights etc, possibly making it difficult to recognise other vessels' lights.
   - The state of wind and sea, and nearness of navigational dangers.
   - Your draught in relation to the depth of water.

   NOTE: The use of radar may be considered as a factor for increased safe speed, but this must depend on exisiting radar operating conditions. These are detailed in Rule *6(a)(b)*.

5. The Rules require a proper look-out, not only by sight, but by hearing as well, and by 'all available means' which includes radar, if fitted. Clearly this specially applies in fog. [*5*]

6. Any action by the 'give-way' vessel must be made in **good time** and be **positive**. In other words, it must be **immediately apparent** to the other vessel that she **is** giving way. [*8(a)(b)*]

7. The 'stand-on' vessel is required to maintain her course and speed, and may confuse things if she does not do so. However, if it appears doubtful that the 'give-way' vessel is taking proper action, then the 'stand-on' vessel may alter course and/or speed herself. This would also be an instance requiring the need for sound signals. [17(b)]

8. The Rules say "A vessel 'constrained by her draught' is a power vessel which, because of her draught in relation to the available depth and width of navigable water, is severely restricted in her ability to deviate from the course she is following". [3(h)]

9. A vessel 'not under command' is one which is unable to manoeuvre as required by the Rules because of an exceptional circumstance, such as an engine or steering breakdown. [3(f)]

10. A long blast (more correctly a 'prolonged blast') should be from four to six seconds duration, and a short blast about one second duration. [32(c)(b)]

11. A vessel that is 'restricted in her ability to manoeuvre' is one whose work means that she is unable to keep out of the way of another vessel. Such vessels include:

    - A vessel laying or picking up navigation marks, submarine cables or pipelines.
    - Vessels dredging, surveying or engaged in underwater operations.
    - Vessels engaged in replenishment of cargo, fuel or persons while under way.
    - A vessel engaged in launching or recovery of aircraft.
    - A vessel engaged in mine clearance operations.
    - A tug whose tow restricts her ability, and the ability of her tow, to deviate from their course. [3(g)]

1. In trying to determine the risk of collision with another vessel, what two considerations need to be taken into account?

2. Technically speaking, when is one vessel said to be overtaking another?

3. When does an overtaking vessel cease to be considered as 'overtaking'?

4. A fast sailing vessel is overtaking a power vessel. Who should give way?

5. While in general, 'power gives way to sail', there are certain types of vessel under power to which a yacht under sail must give way, or situations where she must not impede the other vessel. Can you name five of these?

6. Which of these two sailing vessels has the right of way?

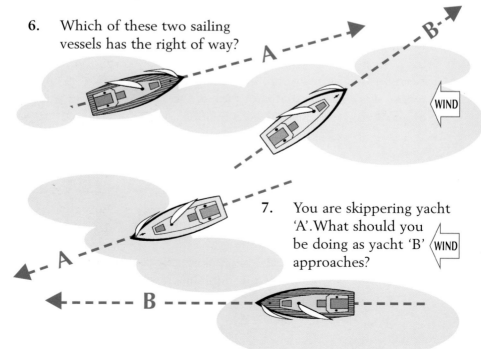

7. You are skippering yacht 'A'. What should you be doing as yacht 'B' approaches?

8. Aboard yacht 'A' you see yacht 'B' approaching. Because of her spinnaker you cannot be sure which tack she is on. What should you do?

9. Which vessel has the right of way in this situation?

10. You are under sail in a small yacht when you sight a large power vessel some way off, but heading directly towards you. What should you do?

11. In this basic situation, how should vessel 'B' alter course? If a sound signal is required, which would be the correct one to use?

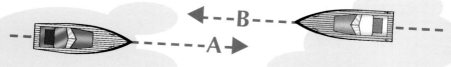

12. If one vessel is obliged by the Rules to give way to another, what are the important points to remember about how she should give way?

13. If you hear a sound signal of three short blasts – what does it mean?

14. What do five or more short blasts indicate?

1. There is a risk of collision if the compass bearing of one vessel from another remains unchanged, or barely changed, and they are getting closer. The Rules say that if there is any doubt about the risk of a collision, then the risk exists! [*7(d)(a)*] This rule needs studying carefully when operating radar.

2. Technically one vessel is said to be overtaking another when she is coming from a direction of more than 22.5 degrees abaft the other's beam. This would mean that, at night, the overtaking vessel would see the stern light of the vessel being overtaken but be unable to see either of her sidelights. [*13(b)(c)*] If in doubt assume that you are overtaking.

3. The overtaking vessel has the duty of keeping clear of the overtaken vessel until she is 'finally past and clear'. This is an example of common sense taking precedence over a precisely worded rule. [*13(d)*]

4. *Any* overtaking vessel must keep clear of the vessel being overtaken, so the yacht must keep clear. [*13(a)*]

5. A vessel under sail must keep clear of:
    - A vessel not under command.
    - A vessel engaged in fishing.
    - A vessel restricted in her ability to manoeuvre.
    - A vessel constrained by her draught. [*18(b)(d)*]
    - Any vessel being overtaken. [*13(a)*]
    - A vessel that can only navigate within the confines of a narrow channel. [*9(b)*]
    - A power vessel following a traffic lane. [*10(j)*]

6. Both yachts are on the same tack, but the windward yacht 'B', must keep clear of yacht 'A'. [*12(a)(ii)*]

7. Boat 'B' is on starboard tack and therefore has right of way. You should head up to wind and pass under her stern. [*12(a)(i)*]

8. Yacht 'A' must give way by turning up to windward and tacking if necessary. A vessel on port tack must give way to another to windward when she is unable to decide which tack the other boat is on. This often happens when the other boat's mainsail is hidden behind a spinnaker. [*12(a)(iii)*]

9. Vessel 'B', as a power boat, should give way to vessel 'A', a sailing boat. Vessel 'A' should hold her course and speed, but be alert to take avoiding action should vessel 'B' fail to take avoiding action and therefore a collision looks likely.

10. Nominally, unless she is displaying any special signal such as 'a vessel constrained by her draught', the other vessel should keep clear of you. But if there is any doubt as to whether she has seen you, it might be wise to alter course to take you well clear. Any change of course should be made **boldly** and **in good time**, so that if the on-coming vessel has seen you she will know you have altered course. Rule 2 emphasises the need for good seamanship and common sense on certain occasions.

11. In a head-on situation with power vessels, each vessel has the responsibility to alter course to starboard to pass down the other's port side. A sound signal of one short blast is appropriate in this situation. [*14(a)*]

12. Any avoiding action required by the Rules should be **positive** and made in **ample time** and the effectiveness of the action carefully checked. [*8(a)*]

13. Three short blasts means 'I am operating astern propulsion'. The vessel has not necessarily started to move astern. [*34(a)*]

14. Five or more short blasts by one vessel in sight of another means 'your intentions are unclear' – or more succinctly, 'What the hell are you doing?' [*34(d)*]

W hen you are afloat, the essential point about being able to recognise any vessel by the shape it displays – whether it is simply a vessel at anchor or one that is fishing – is not only knowing what type of vessel she is but also what she is doing.

It is not good enough just knowing what a tug with a tow looks like; you should know what action you may have to take should you meet one at sea!

1. In daylight, how should a vessel indicate that she is at anchor?

2. How do the Rules apply to smaller craft at anchor?

3. You sight a dredger working in a river. Which signals indicate the clear side on which you should pass?

4. A small craft is showing this rigid flag. What does it mean and what should you do if you are sailing nearby?

5. You see a tug with a tow that appears to be low in the water. How can you tell where the end of the tow is?

6. Why is the same tug also displaying a diamond shape?

7. You are under sail in daylight when the wind drops and you turn on your engine. How should you indicate that you are now a 'power' vessel?

8. What do the shapes displayed by these vessels mean? And what action may you need to take if you are sailing nearby?

A – This vessel is showing two balls.

E – This vessel is showing a cylinder.

B – Here there is a ball at the masthead and one at each yard arm.

F – This vessel is showing three vertical balls.

C – What is the basic meaning of this ball-diamond-ball signal and what types of vessel may show these shapes?

G – This vessel is showing two cones forward and a single cone aft.

D – Two cones hoisted vertically with their points together.

H – If you have to pass this vessel, which side is clear?

1. By hoisting a black anchor ball forward where it can best be seen. [30(a)(i)]

2. Vessels under 7 metres are not obliged to show an anchor ball, unless anchored close to a fairway, narrow channel or an anchorage where other craft are moving. [30(e)]

3. The clear side is indicated by two vertical diamond shapes. Two vertical balls indicate the obstructed side. [27(d)(ii)]

4. Flag 'A' indicates that the vessel is engaged in diving operations and all vessels should keep well clear at slow speed and keep a sharp look-out. [27(e)(ii)]

5. A diamond shape is displayed as near as possible to the rear of the object being towed. [24(g)(iv)]

6. The diamond shape indicates that the overall length of the tug and its tow exceeds 200 metres. [24(a)(v)]

7. Correctly, a sailing vessel proceeding under sail but also being propelled by her engine should display a conical shape, point down, forward of her mast. This is rarely practiced, but it is in the Rules. [25(e)]

8.   **A** – A vessel not under command – most likely due to a mechanical or steering failure. As she cannot manoeuvre as required by the Rules, other vessels **must** keep clear. [27(a)]

    B – This vessel is engaged in mine clearance operations or exercises. It is dangerous to approach within 1000 metres. [27(f)]

    C – This vessel is **restricted in her ability to manoeuvre**. This can apply to several types of vessel – dredgers, tugs with tows, cable laying vessels. These vessels cannot get out of your way, so you **must** keep clear of them. These shapes may also be shown by a vessel at anchor. [27(b)(c)(d)]

    D – This is a fishing vessel engaged either in trawling or another type of fishing. [26(b)(c)]

    E – The cylinder indicates that this vessel's movements are **constrained by her draught**. She may not be able to move away from the middle of a narrow channel. [28]

    F – This signal, three balls, means that the vessel is aground. Could be described as a combination of 'at anchor' and 'not under command'. [30(d)]

    G – Two cones, points together, indicate that this is a fishing vessel. The single cone aft shows that her gear extends for more than 150 metres from the vessel in the direction of the cone. A wise seaman will always keep well clear of fishing vessels. [26(b)]

    H – This dredger shows the 'ball-diamond-ball' signal for a vessel restricted in her ability to manoeuvre. The two vertical diamonds indicate the side on which it is clear to pass, and the two balls show the obstructed side. [27(d)]

15

SECTION 4 • SAILING AT NIGHT

When sailing at night, your first concern must be that your own vessel is showing the appropriate lights.

Next it is important to be able to recognise the lights shown by all other vessels and realise the direction in which they are heading. And, as with daylight signals, you must not only know the lights shown by 'special vessels', but you must also understand how they may affect you and consider whether you should take any action.

NOTE: References to the Rules in the answers to this section relate to the relevant section in the Rules on Lights rather than any Steering and Sailing Rules.

1. What lights should a dinghy under oars be showing at night?

2. Your recently acquired sailing yacht has a tri-colour lantern at the masthead. When can you use it?

3. Although there are some variations, what basic navigation lights should all vessels carry?

4. Correctly, when should you be showing your navigation lights?

5. It is hard to know exactly from what distance your own navigation lights are visible, but where can you find out what their range should be?

6. What lights should a power boat below 12 metres display?

7. Your inflatable tender can probably do around twelve knots. What lights should she display at night?

8. What is the largest vessel that is permitted to show red and green sidelights in one combined lantern?

9. A sailing vessel under 7 metres overall is not, by the Rules, compelled to show navigation lights (although she is strongly advised to do so), so what should she show if the risk of collision occurs?

10. Any vessel may show a second masthead light, with the aft light higher than the forward light. What size vessels *have* to show a second masthead light?

11. As a matter of emergency, your yacht takes another yacht in tow at night. Are there any special lights that you should show?

12. These are the lights of vessels which you may sight at sea. In each case, what type of vessel is indicated by the lights, and in which relative direction is she headed? The text and sketch indicate whether you are under sail or power, and in which relative direction you sight the lights. So – what action, if any, should you take?

A – You are under sail, close-hauled on the port tack when these lights are seen on your starboard beam.

B – Reaching under sail you sight these lights ahead.

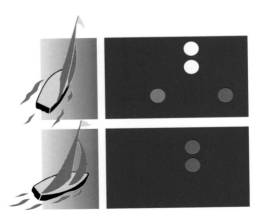

Answers: Sailing at Night

1. At night a dinghy under oars should always carry an electric torch or white lantern which can be used in time to prevent a collision. [25(d)(ii)]

2. Provided your yacht is under 20 metres long, you may use the combined masthead lantern at any time when you are underway but not under power. [25(b)]

3. A masthead light (or two masthead lights if the vessel is over 50 metres), side lights and a stern light. A masthead light is not shown by a vessel under sail. [21(a)(b)]

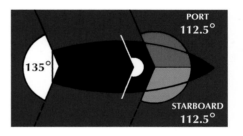

4. Your navigation lights should be switched on: (a) from sunset to sunrise, (b) in poor visibility, and (c) at any other time that the skipper thinks necessary. [20(b)(c)]

5. Less than 12 metres:
Masthead light	2 miles
Sidelights	1 mile
Sternlight	1 mile

   12 metres or more:
Masthead light	5 miles (3 miles if under 20 metres)
Sidelights	2 miles
Sternlight	2 miles [22(b)]

   NB: Knowing where to find these details is more important than knowing them by heart. Details can be found in Rule 22.

6. A power boat under 12 metres may show sidelights and an all-round white light instead of masthead and sternlights. [23(c)(i)]

7. Correctly, a power-driven vessel under 7 metres, but whose maximum speed exceeds 7 knots should carry sidelights and an all-round white light. [23(c){i)]

8. Red and green sidelights may be displayed in a combined lantern only in vessels under 20 metres in length. [25(b)]

9. A powerful electric torch or white hand lantern. [25(d)]

10. Vessels of 50 metres in length or over. [23(a)(ii)]

11. As your yacht is not a regular towing vessel you are not expected to display special lights. But you should, if necessary, be able to indicate to other craft that you have a tow – this may involve shining a powerful light on to the towline. [24(i)]

12. A – This is probably a vessel over 50 metres approaching head on. You should watch her masthead light for any change of course and monitor her compass bearing for a substantial change. You are the stand-on vessel and hopefully are passing ahead of the other vessel. [23(a)]

B – This is a vessel not under command and not making way – typically she may have a mechanical or steering breakdown. She cannot get out of your way so you must keep clear. [27(a)]

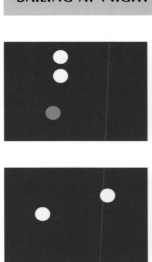 

C – Running under sail you sight these lights on your port bow.

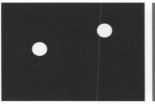 

D – You sight these lights ahead of you as you approach harbour under power.

E – Under sail on the starboard tack, you see these lights on your starboard bow.

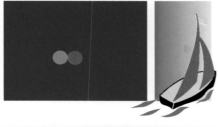

F – You are beating on the port tack when these lights appear on your port bow.

G – While under power you see these lights on your starboard bow.

H – These lights are sighted ahead of you.

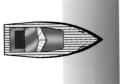

I – Approaching the coast under power, you see these lights ahead of you.

J – You see these lights on your port bow and getting closer.

K – You see these lights ahead and they are getting closer.

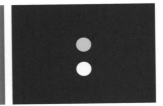

L – These lights appear to be crossing ahead of you.

C – This is a tug with a tow (which does not exceed 200 metres) moving left to right. While she is not, strictly speaking, showing lights saying 'I am restricted in my ability to manoeuvre' you should still keep clear. When confronted with a tug and a tow you must always look out for the end of the tow. [24(a)]

D – She is a vessel at anchor, longer than 50 metres. The lower light is at her stern. Obviously you should keep clear of her. [30(a)(b)]

E – This is a vessel under power, under 50 metres long, and moving from right to left across your bows. Being under sail you have the right of way. Watch out in case she has not seen you. [23(a)]

F – The absence of a mast-head light shows the vessel is under sail and heading towards you. It seems that she is on the port tack and, as the windward vessel, she should give way. But if there is any doubt about which tack she is on, and there is the risk of a collision, you must give way. [25(a)]

G – This is a vessel under sail as it shows no masthead light. It is crossing your course from right to left. You are the vessel under power, so if there is any risk of collision, you must take avoiding action. [25(a)]

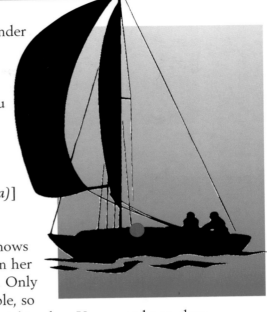

H – Red-white-red shows the vessel is limited in her ability to manoeuvre. Only her stern light is visible, so you appear to be overtaking her. You must keep clear, regardless of whether you are under sail or power. [27(b)]

I – This vessel is aground showing two red 'not under command' lights, but also an anchor light. Obviously you must keep clear and no doubt check the depth of water beneath you! [30(d)]

J – This vessel is fishing, but not making way. You must keep well clear. [27(c)]

K – This is a tug with a tow, seen from astern. The yellow towing light is the clue. Care would be needed here because the tug's tow would be between you and the tug. [24]

L – This is a mine clearance vessel either operating or exercising. She is showing green lights at her masthead and at each yard arm, as well as her navigation lights. Keep at least 1000 metres clear! [27(f)]

M – You are sailing on the starboard tack. These lights are on your starboard beam and seem to be staying the same distance off.

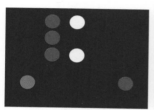

N – While making your way up a buoyed channel under power, you see these lights approaching from astern.

O – While under sail, these lights appear on your starboard bow.

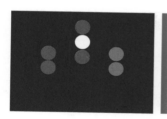

P – Motoring round a bend in a narrow channel, you are suddenly confronted by these lights.

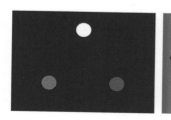

Q – You are running under a spinnaker when these lights appear ahead of you.

R – Close-hauled on the port tack these lights appear fine on the starboard bow.

S – Reaching towards a busy channel from seawards you see these lights on your port bow.

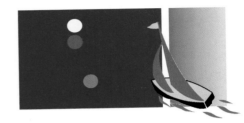

T – You are under sail when these lights approach from astern and appear to be closing.

U – While reaching on the port tack, these lights are sighted on the port bow.

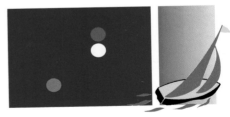

V – While you are under power you sight these lights ahead of you.

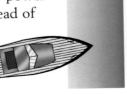

M – Here is a tug with a tow moving from right to left. The key is the three white masthead lights. Further to the right the sidelight of the vessel being towed can be seen. The tug appears to be on a course nearly parallel to you. You should keep a careful watch and keep well clear. [24]

N – The three vertical red lights show that this is a vessel constrained by its draught and the two masthead lights show it to be over 50 metres. The aspect of the masthead lights and sidelights show that she is following you. You should move as far as possible to the starboard side of the channel to allow her enough room to pass on your port side. [28]

O – This is a fishing vessel – green over white shows her to be trawling. Her other navigation lights show her to be making way and moving from left to right. Other vessels should keep clear and not pass too close because of her nets astern. [26(b)]

P – This is a dredger at work. She shows the red-white-red lights of a vessel restricted in her ability to manoeuvre. The two vertical green lights show the side of the vessel on which it is clear to pass, while the two vertical red lights show the obstructed side. These red and green lights are all-round lights. [27(d)]

Q – This is a power vessel under 50 metres long approaching you bows on. She should give way to you if it is necessary, but you should watch her carefully to ensure that she has seen you – and remember that with a spinnaker you may not be able to alter course very quickly. [23(a)(ii)]

R – This is a vessel under power and under 50 metres in length crossing your path from right to left. You have the right of way, but it looks as if she will pass clear ahead of you. [23(a)(ii)]

S – This is a Pilot vessel on duty – white over red – and moving from left to right. If necessary she must give way to you. [29]

T – This is not quite straightforward. The three masthead lights show that this is a tug with a tow over 200m, and the red-white-red indicates a vessel limited in ability to manoeuvre. Although under any other circumstances you should keep clear, Rule 13 states that an overtaking vessel shall keep clear of a vessel being overtaken, regardless of other rules. Nevertheless, it still would be prudent (and legal) for you to move out of the way providing **it is quite clear to the tug that you are doing so**. See Rule 2.

U – This is a fishing vessel, not trawling (red over white) and under way moving from left to right. You must keep clear. [26(c)(i)]

V – You are catching up with a fishing vessel that is trawling – green over white and carrying a white stern light. You must keep well clear as she may have gear out astern. [26(b)]

SECTION 5 • NARROW CHANNELS

1. What is the definition of a narrow channel?

2. What basic instruction should be observed by all vessels, whether sail or power, that are navigating in a narrow channel?

3. In narrow channels what special instructions should be observed by power craft under 20 metres long and all sailing vessels?

4. A vessel wishes to overtake another in a narrow channel, passing the leading vessel on the port side. If she feels it is necessary to warn the vessel ahead, what sound signal should she give?

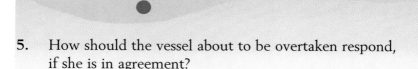

5. How should the vessel about to be overtaken respond, if she is in agreement?

6. There are important rules governing Traffic Separation Schemes. How can you tell where these Schemes operate, and if you are in one?

7. In a Traffic Separation Scheme, how or where should you join one of the traffic lanes?

8. How is the behaviour of sailing vessels affected by the rules concerning an Inshore Traffic Zone?

9. These two yachts are crossing a Traffic Separation Scheme. Which one is doing it correctly and why?

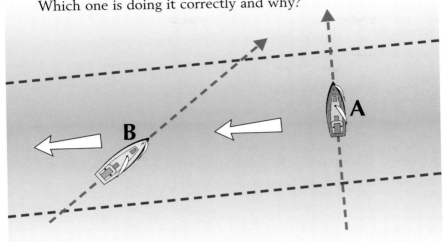

10. Your small sailing yacht is in one of the lanes in a Traffic Separation Scheme. Are you allowed to sail in the opposite direction to the main flow in that lane?

11. What is this area called?

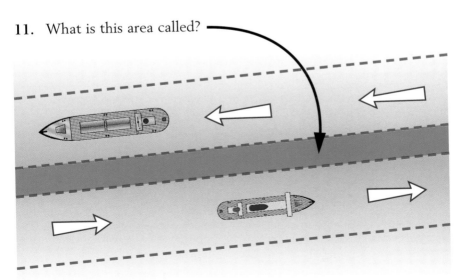

1. There is no precise definition of a narrow channel in the Rules. In practical terms any fairway or buoyed channel leading to a port or harbour may technically be thought of as a 'narrow channel'. What may seem wide to a small yacht will be relatively narrow for a big ship.

2. Any vessel navigating in a narrow channel must keep over as far as possible to the starboard side of the channel. In other words – keep to the right. [9(a)]

3. Power craft under 20 metres and sailing vessels shall not impede any other vessel in a narrrow channel. [9(b)]

4. Two long blasts followed by two short blasts (port side). [34(c)]

5. If the vessel agrees to be overtaken, she sounds one long blast and one short blast, followed by one long blast and one short blast. [34(c)]

6. Details of all Traffic Separation Schemes are shown on all large scale charts, and in major almanacs.

7. If possible, join at the start or termination of the lane, but otherwise join it at as small an angle as possible to the general direction of traffic flow. [10(b)(iii)]

8. Sailing vessels (and vessels under 20 metres) may use the Inshore Zones at any time. [*10(d)(i)*]

9. Yacht 'A' is doing it correctly. Vessels crossing a traffic lane (if obliged to do so) should cross on a heading as nearly as practicable at right angles to the general flow of traffic, regardless of wind or tide. This makes them as visible as possible to oncoming traffic. A yacht under sail unable to comply with this should consider crossing under power. [*10(c)*]

10. Under no circumstances may any vessel sail in the oppposite direction to the main flow of traffic in any lane. [*10(b)*]

11. It is a Traffic Separation Zone, dividing two traffic lanes. All vessels should, as far as possible, keep clear of a Traffic Separation Zone. [*10(b)*]

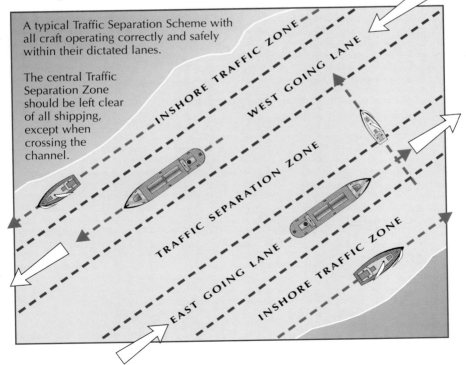

A typical Traffic Separation Scheme with all craft operating correctly and safely within their dictated lanes.

The central Traffic Separation Zone should be left clear of all shippjng, except when crossing the channel.

INSHORE TRAFFIC ZONE

WEST GOING LANE

TRAFFIC SEPARATION ZONE

EAST GOING LANE

INSHORE TRAFFIC ZONE

SECTION 6 • FOG & POOR VISIBILITY

1. You have a 10 metre sailing yacht. What are the rules about the way you should make sound signals in fog or poor visibility?

2. When a vessel is sailing in fog, without the use of her engine, what sound signal should she be making?

3. Will the circumstances change if she decides to turn on her motor?

4. While you are in fog, you hear a vessel sounding two prolonged blasts at about two minute intervals. What does this tell you?

5. Again, while you are in fog, you are surprised to hear the sound of a gong. What would this indicate?

6. If you hear one long blast followed by two short blasts, what type of vessel is making the signal?

7. Immediately after hearing one long and two short blasts, you hear one long blast followed by three short blasts. What do the signals tell you and what sort of action might you need to take?

8. You have anchored in fog well inshore in your 10 metre yacht. What additional sound signal should you make?

9. You are at anchor in fog and making the correct sound signals. You hear another vessel approaching – what additional sound signal should you make?

10. You are in a 10 metre power boat under way and making way in fog. The boat is equipped with a fog horn. What sound signal should you be making?

11. In this same power boat, while under way in fog you decide to stop. What sound signal should you be making?

12. You are unlucky enough to run aground in fog. What sound signal should you be making to indicate your situation?

13. Whereas you have no visual contact with a nearby vessel in the fog, you can hear a sound signal indicating a power vessel under way. The vessel is also making four short blasts after one long blast. What is the she up to?

14. In poor visibility you hear a fog signal somewhere ahead. What shoud you do?

1. A vessel under 12 metres is not obliged to carry a fog horn (whistle) and a bell or make the prescribed signals with these. But if she does not, she must make some other efficient sound signal at intervals of not less than two minutes. [35(i)]

2. A sailing vessel under way in fog should sound one long blast and two short blasts at intervals of not more than two minutes. [35(c)]

    less than 2 minutes

3. If the vessel turns on her engine, even though her sails are still hoisted, she becomes a power vessel making way through the water and should sound one long blast every two minutes. [35(a)]

    2 minutes

    2 minutes

4. She is a power vessel that is under way, but stopped and making no way through the water. [35(b)]

5. A vessel at anchor and over 100 metres in length should both sound a bell up forward and beat a gong rapidly for five seconds at one minute intervals in the aft part of the vessel. [35(g)]

6. One long and two short blasts is the signal made by vessels that are generally limited in their ability to manoeuvre. This includes sailing vessels, vessels not under command, fishing vessels, and tugs with tows. [35(c)]

7. One long blast and three short blasts are sounded by a vessel under tow, which indicates that the previous one long blast and two short blasts were sounded by the tug. [35(e)]

    NOTE: When close to tugs, you should always ensure that you are well clear of their tow.

8. You should ring your bell rapidly for about five seconds at intervals of not more than one minute. But strictly

Ring bell for 5 seconds every minute

speaking, a vessel under 12 metres is allowed to make 'some other efficient sound signal' at intervals of not more than two minutes. (This could include giving one short blast, a long blast, and a short blast on your foghorn to warn other vessels in the vicinity of your position.) [35(g)]

9. One short blast, one long blast and one short blast (Morse Code R) sounded on a fog horn may be used as an additional warning. [35(g)]

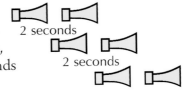

(Morse Code R)

10. You should be sounding a prolonged blast at least every two minutes. [35(a)]

Every 2 minutes

11. If you stop and are not making way through the water, you should sound two long blasts in succession, with an interval of about two seconds between them. [35(b)]

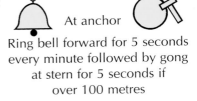

2 seconds

2 seconds

12. Vessels aground sound a bell as at anchor, but also make three separate and distinct strokes of the bell before and after the rapid ringing. [35(h)]

At anchor

Ring bell forward for 5 seconds every minute followed by gong at stern for 5 seconds if over 100 metres

13. She is a pilot vessel on duty. [35(j)]

14. Reduce speed to the minimum necessary to keep steerage way, and navigate with extreme caution until the danger of collision is over. This, of course, includes making your own sound signals. [19(e)]

SECTION 7 • A MIXED BAG

NOTE: There are a few questions here concerning distress signals. While distress signals are not strictly part of the Rule of the Road, they are in fact covered by an annex to the Rules.

1. You see someone standing on a small boat raising and lowering his arms. What is he trying to indicate?

2. A vessel is said to be 'under way, but not making way'. What actually is she doing?

3. In this situation in a buoyed channel the yacht is under sail. What action should she take?

4. How can you indicate distress with a fog horn?

5. Although not covered by the Rules how, at night, can a yacht draw attention to her position if she thinks another vessel has not seen her and a collision is possible?

6. By day, how would you indicate distress, and your position, to a rescue helicopter?

7. Is *securité* a distress signal?

8. You see this single white light, fairly close, when you are offshore. What might it be?

9. You have to make a MAYDAY call. What information should be given when the call is made?

10. You are under power in a buoyed channel leading into a port. Looking aft you see a ferry following you up the channel, and probably needing to pass you. What should you do?

11. What lights are shown by a small vessel supporting a night dive?

12. What is the correct arc of visibility of a masthead light?

13. At night, in your sailing yacht, you have just turned on your motor to help you along. What do you need to do about your navigation lights?

14. If you start using your motor for propulsion while you are still under sail, apart from navigation lights at night, what else do you need to do to comply with the Rules?

15. You sight these lights: the yellow light is flashing. What is the vessel and which way is she heading?

1. This is a distress signal and the person needs help. [*Annex IV 1.(k)*]

2. 'Under way, but not making way' means not anchored nor moored but not moving through the water.

3. The yacht must not impede the progress of the power vessel. She should keep to the starboard side of the buoyed channel, and if there is sufficient depth of water, possibly sail outside the channel.

4. Sounding a fog horn continuously. [*Annex IV(b)*]

5. She may shine a powerful white light on her sails – not at the approaching vessel as this could easily dazzle the watchkeeper. Or she may fire a white flare (which is not a distress signal) to draw attention to her position. NOTE: If ever you fire a white flare you should always inform the nearest coastguard in case it is mistakenly reported as a distress signal.

6. By using an orange smoke flare. [*Annex IV(j)*]

7. No. It is a safety signal normally used by shore stations before broadcasting an important navigation or meteorological warning.

8. It is most likely to be the stern light of a vessel, but it could, in theory, be a light shown by a sailing vessel under 7 metres that chooses not to show normal navigation lights.

9. The vessel's name, position, nature of distress, assistance required, and the number of people on board.

10. Move over as far as possible to the side of the channel on your starboard hand. If the depth of water allows, you may consider sailing outside the marked channel.

11. Three vertical lights,
    red-white-red, where they
    can best be seen. [27(e)(i)]

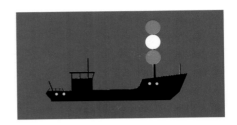

12. The total arc is 225 degrees,
    fixed so as to show from
    right ahead to 22.5 degrees
    abaft the beam on either
    side. [21(a)]

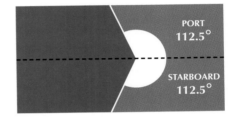

13. Your yacht is now a 'power
    vessel'. Your masthead light
    must be switched on,
    together with your sidelights.
    A combined lantern is no
    longer appropriate.

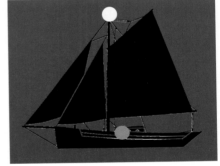

14. Again, your yacht is now a
    'power vessel', even though
    your sails may still be hoisted.
    You must follow the Steering
    and Sailing Rules that apply
    to power vessels rather than
    vessels under sail.

15. The flashing yellow light
    indicates a hovercraft and
    she is moving left to right.
    You are looking at her
    starboard bow.

THE INTERNATIONAL REGULATIONS FOR PREVENTING COLLISIONS AT SEA

PART A. GENERAL

RULE 1 APPLICATION

(a) These Rules shall apply to all vessels upon the high seas and in all waters connected therewith navigable by seagoing vessels.

(b) Nothing in these Rules shall interfere with the operation of special rules made by an appropriate authority for roadsteads, harbours, rivers, lakes or inland waterways connected with the high seas and navigable by seagoing vessels. Such special rules shall conform as closely as possible to these Rules.

(c) Nothing in these Rules shall interfere with the operation of any special rules made by the Government of any State with respect to additional station or signal lights, shapes or whistle signals for ships of war and vessels proceeding under convoy, or with respect to additional station or signal lights or shapes for fishing vessels engaged in fishing as a fleet. These additional station or signal lights, shapes or whistle signals shall, so far as possible, be such that they cannot be mistaken for any light, shape or signal authorised elsewhere under these Rules.

(d) Traffic separation schemes may be adopted by the Organisation for the purpose of these Rules.

(e) Whenever the Government concerned shall have determined that a vessel of special construction or purpose cannot comply fully with the provisions of any of these Rules with respect to the number, position, range or arc of visibility of lights or shapes, as well as to the disposition and characteristics of sound-signalling appliances, such vessel shall comply with such other provisions in regard to the number, position, range of arc of visibility of lights or shapes, as well as to the disposition and characteristics of sound-signalling appliances, as her Government shall have determined to be the closest possible compliance with these Rules in respect of that vessel.

RULE 2 RESPONSIBILITY

(a) Nothing in these Rules shall exonerate any vessel, or the owner, master or crew thereof, from the consequences of any neglect to comply with these Rules or of the neglect of any precaution which may be required by the ordinary practice of seamen, or by the special circumstances of the case.

(b) In construing and complying with these Rules due regard shall be had to all dangers of navigation and collision and to any special circumstances, including the limitations of the vessels involved, which may make a departure. from these Rules necessary to avoid immediate danger.

RULE 3 GENERAL DEFINITIONS

For the purpose of these Rules, except where the context otherwise requires:

(a) The word "vessel" includes every description of water craft, including non-displacement craft and seaplanes, used or capable of being used as a means of transportation on water.

(b) The term "power-driven vessel" means any vessel propelled by machinery.

(c) The term "sailing vessel" means any vessel under sail provided that propelling machinery, if fitted, is not being used.

(d) The term "vessel engaged in fishing" means any vessel fishing with nets, lines, trawls or other fishing apparatus which restrict manoeuvrability, but does not include a vessel fishing with trolling lines or other fishing apparatus which do not restrict manoeuvrability.

(e) The word "seaplane" includes any aircraft designed to manoeuvre on the water.

(f) The term "vessel not under command" means a vessel which through some exceptional circumstances is unable to manoeuvre as required by these Rules and is therefore unable to keep out of the way of another vessel.

(g) The term "vessel restricted in her ability to manoeuvre" means a vessel which from the nature of her work is restricted in her ability to manoeuvre as required by these Rules and is therefore unable to keep out of the way of another vessel.

The term "vessels restricted in their ability to manoeuvre" shall include but not be limited to:

(i) a vessel engaged in laying, servicing or picking up a navigation mark, submarine cable or pipeline;

(ii) a vessel engaged in dredging, surveying or underwater operations;

(iii) a vessel engaged in replenishment or transferring persons, provisions or cargo while underway;

(iv) a vessel engaged in the launching or recovery of aircraft;

(v) a vessel engaged in mine-clearance operations;

(vi) a vessel engaged in a towing operation such as severely restricts the towing vessel and her tow in their ability to deviate from their course.

(h) The term "vessel constrained by her draught" means a power-driven vessel which. because of her draught in relation to the available depth and width of navigable water, is severely restricted in her ability to deviate from the course she is following.

(i) The word "underway" means that a vessel is not at anchor, or made fast to the shore, or aground.

(j) The words "length" and "breadth" of a vessel mean her length overall and greatest breadth.

(k) Vessels shall be deemed to be in sight of one another only when one can be observed visually from the other.

(l) The term "restricted visibility" means any condition in which visibility is restricted by fog, mist, falling snow, heavy rainstorms, sandstorms or any other similar causes.

PART B. STEERING & SAILING RULES

Section 1: Conduct of vessels in any condition of visibility

RULE 4 APPLICATION

Rules in this Section apply in any condition of visibility.

RULE 5 LOOK-OUT

Every vessel shall at all times maintain a proper look-out by sight and hearing as well as by all available means appropriate in the prevailing circumstances and conditions so as to make a full appraisal of the situation and of the risk of collision.

RULE 6 SAFE SPEED

Every vessel shall at all times proceed at a safe speed so that she can take proper and effective action to avoid collision and be stopped within a distance appropriate to the prevailing circumstances and conditions.

In determining a safe speed the following factors shall be among those taken into account:

(a) By all vessels:
(i) the state of visibility;
(ii) the traffic density including concentrations of fishing vessels or any other vessels;
(iii) the manoeuvrability of the vessel with special reference to stopping distance and turning ability in the prevailing conditions;
(iv) at night the presence of background light such as from shore lights or from back scatter of her own lights;
(v) the state of wind, sea and current, and the proximity of navigational hazards;
(vi) the draught in relation to the available depth of water.

(b) Additionally, by vessels with operational radar;
(i) the characteristics, efficiency and limitations of the radar equipment;
(ii) any constraints imposed by the radar range scale in use;
(iii) the effect on radar detection of the sea state, weather and other sources of interference;
(iv) the possibility that small vessels, ice and other floating objects may not be detected by radar at an adequate range;
(v) the number, location and movement of vessels detected by radar;
(vi) the more exact assessment of the visibility that may be possible when radar is used to determine the range of vessels or other objects in the vicinity.

RULE 7 RISK OF COLLISION

(a) Every vessel shall use all available means appropriate to the prevailing circumstances and conditons to determine if risk of collision exists. If there is any doubt such risk shall be deemed to exist.
(b) Proper use shall be made of radar equipment if fitted and operational, including long-range scanning to obtain early warning of risk of collision and radar plotting or equivalent systematic observation of detected objects.
(c) Assumptions shall not be made on the basis of scanty information, especially scanty radar information.
(d) In determining if risk of collision exists the following considerations shall be among those taken into account:
(i) such risk shall be deemed to exist if the compass bearing of an approaching vessel does not appreciably change;
(ii) such risk may sometimes exist even when an appreciable bearing change is evident, particularly when approaching a very large vessel or a tow or when approaching a vessel at close range.

RULE 8 ACTION TO AVOID COLLISION

(a) Any action taken to avoid collision shall, if the circumstances of the case admit, be positive, made in ample time and with due regard to the observance of good seamanship.

(b) Any alteration of course and/or speed to avoid collision shall, if the circumstances of the case admit, be large enough to be readily apparent to another vessel observing visually or by radar; a succession of small alterations of course and/or speed should be avoided.
(c) If there is sufficient sea room, alteration of course alone may be the most effective action to avoid a close-quarters situation provided that it is made in good time, is substantial and does not result in another close-quarters situation.
(d) Action taken to avoid collision with another vessel shall be such as to result in passing at a safe distance. The effectiveness of the action shall be carefully checked until the other vessel is finally past and clear.
(e) If necessary to avoid collision or allow more time to assess the situation, a vessel shall slacken her speed or take all way off by stopping or reversing her means of propulsion.
(f) (i) A vessel which, by another of these rules, is required not to impede the passage or safe passage of another vessel shall, when required by the circumstances of the case, take early action to allow sufficient sea room for the safe passage of the other vessel;
(ii) A vessel required not to impede the passage or safe passage of another vessel is not relieved of this obligation if approaching the other vessel so as to involve risk of collision and shall, when taking action, have full regard to the action which may be required by the rules of this part.
(iii) A vessel the passage of which is not to be impeded remains fully obliged to comply with the rules of this part when the two vessels are approaching one another so as to involve risk of collision.

RULE 9 NARROW CHANNELS

(a) A vessel proceeding along the course of a narrow channel or fairway shall keep as near to the outer limit of the channel or fairway which lies on her starboard side as is safe and practicable.
(b) A vessel of less than 20 metres in length or a sailing vessel shall not impede the passage of a vessel which can safely navigate only within a narrow channel or fairway.
(c) A vessel engaged in fishing shall not impede the passage of any other vessel navigating within a narrow channel or fairway.
(d) A vessel shall not cross a narrow channel or fairway if such crossing impedes the passage of a vessel which can safely navigate only within such channel or fairway. The latter vessel may use the sound signal prescribed in Rule 34(d) if in doubt as to the intention of the crossing vessel.
(e) (i) In a narrow channel or fairway when overtaking can take place only if the vessel to be overtaken has to take action to permit safe passing, the vessel intending to overtake shall indicate her intention by sounding the appropriate signal prescribed in Rule 34(c) (i). The vessel to be overtaken shall, if in agreement, sound the appropriate signal prescribed in Rule 34(c)(ii) and take steps to permit safe passing. If in doubt she may sound the signals prescribed in Rule 34(d).
(ii) This Rule does not relieve the overtaking vessel of her obligation under Rule 13.
(f) A vessel nearing a bend or an area of a narrow channel or fairway where other vessels may be obscured by an intervening obstruction shall navigate with particular alertness and caution and shall sound the appropriate signal prescribed in Rule 34(e).
(g) Any vessel shall, if the circumstances of the case admit, avoid anchoring in a narrow channel.

41

RULE 10 TRAFFIC SEPARATION SCHEMES

(a) This Rule applies to traffic separation schemes adopted by the Organisation and does not relieve any vessel of her obligation under any other rule.

(b) A vessel using a traffic separation scheme shall:
(i) proceed in the appropriate traffic lane in the general direction of traffic flow for that lane;
(ii) so far as practicable keep clear of a traffic separation line or separation zone;
(iii) normally join or leave a traffic lane at the termination of the lane, but when joining or leaving from either side shall do so at as small an angle to the general direction of traffic flow as practicable.

(c) A vessel shall, so far as practicable, avoid crossing traffic lanes, but if obliged to do so shall cross on a heading as nearly as practicable at right angles to the general direction of traffic flow.

(d) (i) A vessel shall not use an inshore traffic zone when she can safely use the appropriate traffic lane within the traffic separation scheme. However, vessels of less than 20 metres in length, sailing vessels and vessels engaged in fishing may use the inshore traffic zone.
(ii) Notwithstanding sub-paragraph (d) (i), a vessel may use an inshore traffic zone when *en route* to or from a port, offshore installation or structure, pilot station, or any other place situated within the inshore traffic zone or to avoid immediate danger.

(e) A vessel other than a crossing vessel or a vessel joining or leaving a lane shall not normally enter a separation zone or cross a separation line except:
(i) in case of emergency to avoid immediate danger;
(ii) to engage in fishing within a separation zone.

(f) A vessel navigating in areas near the terminations of traffic separation schemes shall do so with particular caution.

(g) A vessel shall so far as practicable avoid anchoring in a traffic separation scheme or in areas near its terminations.

(h) A vessel not using a traffic separation scheme shall avoid it by as wide a margin as is practicable.

(i) A vessel engaged in fishing shall not impede the passage of any vessel following a traffic lane.

(j) A vessel of less than 20 metres in length or a sailing vessel shall not impede the safe passage of a power-driven vessel following a traffic lane.

(k) A vessel restricted in her ability to manoeuvre when engaged in an operation for the maintenance of safety of navigation in a traffic separation scheme is exempted from complying with this Rule to the extent necessary to carry out the operation.

(l) A vessel restricted in her ability to manoeuvre when engaged in an operation for the laying, servicing or picking up of a submarine cable, within a traffic separation scheme, is exempted from complying with this Rule to the extent necessary to carry out the operation.

Section 2: Conduct of vessels in sight of one another

RULE 11 APPLICATION

Rules in this Section apply to vessels in sight of one another.

RULE 12 SAILING VESSELS

(a) When two sailing vessels are approaching one another, so as to involve risk of collision, one of them shall keep out of the way of the other as follows:

(i) when each has the wind on a different side, the vessel which has the wind on the port side shall keep out of the way of the other:
(ii) when both have the wind on the same side, the vessel which is to windward shall keep out of the way of the vessel which is to leeward:
(iii) if a vessel with the wind on the port side sees a vessel to windward and cannot determine with certainty whether the other vessel has the wind on the port or on the starboard side, she shall keep out of the way of the other.

(b) For the purposes ot this Rule the windward side shall be deemed to be the side opposite to that on which the mainsail is carried or, in the case of a square-rigged vessel, the side opposite to that on which the largest fore-and-aft sail is carried.

RULE 13 OVERTAKING

(a) Notwithstanding anything contained in the Rules of Part B, Sections 1 and 2, any vessel overtaking any other shall keep out of the way of the vessel being overtaken.

(b) A vessel shall be deemed to be overtaking when coming up with another vessel from a direction more than 22.5 degrees abaft her beam, that is, in such a position with reference to the vessel she is overtaking, that at night she would be able to see only the sternlight of that vessel but neither of her sidelights.

(c) When a vessel is in any doubt as to whether she is overtaking another, she shall assume that this is the case and act accordingly.

(d) Any subsequent alteration of the bearing between the two vessels shall not make the overtaking vessel a crossing vessel within the meaning of these Rules or relieve her of the duty of keeping clear of the overtaken vessel until she is finally past and clear.

RULE 14 HEAD-ON SITUATION

(a) When two power-driven vessels are meeting on reciprocal or nearly reciprocal courses so as to involve risk of collision each shall alter her course to starboard so that each shall pass on the port side of the other.

(b) Such a situation shall be deemed to exist when a vessel sees the other ahead or nearly ahead and by night she could see the masthead lights of the other in a line or nearly in a line and/or both side-lights and by day she observes the corresponding aspect of the other vessel.

(c) When a vessel is in any doubt as to whether such a situation exists she shall assume that it does exist and act accordingly.

RULE 15 CROSSING SITUATION

When two power-driven vessels are crossing so as to involve risk of collision, the vessel which has the other on her own starboard side shall keep out of the way and shall, if the circumstances of the case admit, avoid crossing ahead of the other vessel.

RULE 16 ACTION BY GIVE-WAY VESSEL

Every vessel which is directed to keep out of the way of another vessel shall, so far as possible, take early and substantial action to keep well clear.

RULE 17 ACTION BY STAND-ON VESSEL

(a)(i) Where one of two vessels is to keep out of the way the other shall keep her course and speed.

(ii) The latter vessel may however take action to avoid collision by her manoeuvre alone, as soon as it becomes apparent to her that the vessel required to keep out of the way is not taking appropriate action in compliance with these Rules.

(b) When, from any cause, the vessel required to keep her course and speed finds herself so close that collision cannot be avoided by the action of the give-way vessel alone, she shall take such action as will best aid to avoid collision.

(c) A power-driven vessel which takes action in a crossing situation in accordance with sub- paragraph (a)(ii) of this Rule to avoid collision with another power-driven vessel shall, if the circumstances of the case admit, not alter course to port for a vessel on her own port side.

(d) This Rule does not relieve the give-way vessel of her obligation to keep out of the way.

RULE 18 RESPONSIBILITIES BETWEEN VESSELS

Except where Rules 9, 10 and 13 otherwise require:
(a) A power-driven vessel underway shall keep out of the way of:
(i) a vessel not under command;
(ii) a vessel restricted in her ability to manoeuvre;
(iii) a vessel engaged in fishing;
(iv) a sailing vessel;
(b) A sailing vessel underway shall keep out of the way of:
(i) a vessel not under command;
(ii) a vessel restricted in her ability to manoeuvre;
(iii) a vessel engaged in fishing.
(c) A vessel engaged in fishing when underway shall as far as possible, keep out of the way of:
(i) A vessel not under command;
(ii) a vessel restricted in her ability to manoeuvre;
(d)(i) Any vessel other than a vessel not under command or a vessel restricted in her ability to manoeuvre shall, if the circumstances of the case admit, avoid impeding the safe passage of a vessel constrained by her draught, exhibiting the signals in Rule 28.
(ii) A vessel constrained by her draft shall navigate with particular caution having full regard to her special condition.
(e) A seaplane on the water shall, in general, keep well clear of all vessels and avoid impeding their navigation. In circumstances, however, where risk of collision exists, she shall comply with the Rules of this Part.

Section 3: Conduct of vessels in restricted visibility

RULE 19 CONDUCT OF VESSELS IN
RESTRICTED VISIBILITY

(a) This Rule applies to vessels not in sight of one another when navigating in or near an area of restricted visibility.
(b) Every vessel shall proceed at a safe speed adapted to the prevailing circumstances and conditions of restricted visibility. A power-driven vessel shall have her engines ready for immediate manoeuvre.
(c) Every vessel shall have due regard to the prevailing circumstances and conditions of restricted visibility when complying with the Rules of Section 1 of this Part.
(d) A vessel which detects by radar alone the presence of

another vessel shall determine if a close-quarters situation is developing and/or risk of collision exists. If so, she shall take avoiding action in ample time, provided that when such action consists of an alteration of course, so far as possible the following shall be avoided:
(i) an alteration of course to port for a vessel forward of the beam, other than for a vessel being overtaken;
(ii) an alteration of course towards a vessel abeam or abaft the beam.
(e) Except where it has been determined that a risk of collision does not exist, every vessel which hears apparently forward of her beam the fog signal of another vessel, or which cannot avoid a close-quarters situation with another vessel forward of her beam, shall reduce her speed to the minimum at which she can be kept on her course. She shall if necessary take all her way off and in any event navigate with extreme caution until danger of collision is over.

RULE 20 APPLICATION

(a) Rules in this Part shall be complied with in all weathers.
(b) The Rules concerning lights shall be complied with from sunset to sunrise, and during such times no other lights shall be exhibited, except such lights as cannot be mistaken for the lights specified in these Rules or do not impair their visibility or distinctive character, or interfere with the keeping of a proper look-out.
(c) The lights prescribed by these Rules shall, if carried, also be exhibited from sunrise to sunset in restricted visibility and may be exhibited in all other circumstances when it is deemed necessary.
(d) The Rules concerning shapes shall be complied with by day.
(e) The lights and shapes specified in these Rules shall comply with the provisions of Annex I to these Regulations.

RULE 21 DEFINITIONS

(a) "Masthead light" means a white light placed over the fore and aft centreline of the vessel showing an unbroken light over an arc of the horizon of 225 degrees and so fixed as to show the light from right ahead to 22.5 degrees abaft the beam on either side of the vessel.
(b) "Sidelights" means a green light on the starboard side and a red light on the port side each showing an unbroken light over an arc of the horizon of 112.5 degrees and so fixed as to show the light from right ahead to 22.5 degrees abaft the beam on its respective side. In a vessel of less than 20 metres in length the sidelights may be combined in one lantern carried on the fore and aft centreline of the vessel.
(c) "Sternlight" means a white light placed as nearly as practicable at the stern showing an unbroken light over an arc of the horizon of 135 degrees and so fixed as to show the light 67.5 degrees from right aft on each side of the vessel.
(d) "Towing light" means a yellow light having the same characteristics as the "sternlight" defined in paragraph (c) of this Rule.
(e) "All round light" means a light showing an unbroken light over an arc of the horizon of 360 degrees.
(f) "Flashing light" means a light flashing at regular intervals at a frequency of 120 flashes or more per minute.

RULE 22 VISIBILITY OF LIGHTS

The lights prescribed in these Rules shall be visible at the following minimum ranges:

(a) In vessels of 50 metres or more in length:
– a masthead light, 6 miles;
– a sidelight, 3 miles;
– a sternlight, 3 miles;
– a towing light, 3 miles;
– a white, red, green or yellow all-round light, 3 miles.
(b) In vessels of 12 metres or more in length but less than 50 metres in length:
– a masthead light, 5 miles; except that where the length of the vessel is less than 20 metres, 3 miles;
– a sidelight, 2 miles;
– a sternlight, 2 miles;
– a towing light, 2 miles;
– a white, red, green or yellow all-round light, 2 miles.
(c) In vessels of less than 12 metres in length:
– a masthead light, 2 miles;
– a sidelight, 1 mile;
– a sternlight, 2 miles;
– a towing light, 2 miles;
– a white, red, green or yellow all-round light, 2 miles.
(d) In inconspicuous, partly submerged vessels or objects being towed:
– a white all-round light, 3 miles.

RULE 23 POWER-DRIVEN VESSELS UNDERWAY

(a) A power-driven vessel underway shall exhibit:
(i) a masthead light forward;
(ii) a second masthead light abaft of and higher than the forward one; except that a vessel of less than 50 metres in length shall not be obliged to exhibit such light but may do so;
(iii) sidelights;
(iv) sternlights.
(b) An air-cushion vessel when operating in the non-displacement mode shall, in addition to the lights prescribed in paragraph (a) of this Rule, exhibit an all-round flashing yellow light.
(c) (i) A power-driven vessel of less than 12 metres in length may in lieu of the lights prescribed in paragraph (a) of this Rule exhibit an all-round white light and sidelights;
(ii) a power-driven vessel of less than 7 metres in length whose maximum speed does not exceed 7 knots may in lieu of the lights prescribed in paragraph (a) of this Rule exhibit an all-round white light and shall, if practicable, also exhibit sidelights;
(iii) the masthead light or all-round white light on a power-driven vessel of less than 12 metres in length may be displaced from the fore and aft centreline of the vessel if centreline fitting is not practicable, provided that the sidelights are combined in one lantern which shall be carried on the fore and aft centreline of the vessel or located as nearly as practicable in the same fore and aft line as the masthead light or the all-round white light.

RULE 24 TOWING AND PUSHING

(a) A power-driven vessel when towing shall exhibit:
(i) instead of the light prescribed in Rule 23(a)(i) or

(a)(ii) two masthead lights forward in a vertical line. When the length of the tow, measuring from the stem of the towing vessel to the after end of the tow exceeds 200 metres, three such lights in a vertical line;
(ii) sidelights;
(iii) a sternlight;
(iv) a towing light in a vertical line above the sternlight;
(v) when the length of the tow exceeds 200 metres, a diamond shape where it can best be seen.
(b) When a pushing vessel and a vessel being pushed ahead are rigidly connected in a composite unit they shall be regarded as a power-driven vessel and exhibit the light prescribed in Rule 23.
(c) A power-driven vessel when pushing ahead or towing alongside, except in the case of a composite unit, shall exhibit:
(i) instead of the light prescribed in Rule 23(a)(i) or (a)(ii), two masthead lights forward in a vertical line
(ii) sidelights;
(iii) a sternlight.
(d) A power-driven vessel to which paragraph (a) or (c) of this Rule applies shall also comply with Rule 23 (a)(ii).
(e) A vessel or object being towed, other than mentioned in paragraph (g) of the Rule, shall exhibit:
(i) sidelights;
(ii) a sternlight;
(iii) when the length of the tow exceeds 200 metres, a diamond shape where it can best be seen.
(f) Provided that any number of vessels being towed alongside or pushed in a group shall be lighted as one vessel;
(i) a vessel being pushed ahead, not being part of a composite unit, shall exhibit at the forward end, sidelights;
(ii) a vessel being towed alongside shall exhibit a sternlight and at the forward end, sidelights.
(g) An inconspicuous partly submerged vessel or object, or combination of such vessels or objects being towed, shall exhibit:
(i) if it is less than 25 metres in breadth, one all-round white light at or near the forward end and one at or near the after end except that dracones need not exhibit a light at or near the forward end;
(ii) if it is 25 metres or more in breadth, two additional all-round white lights at or near the extremities of its breadth;
(iii) If it exceeds 100 metres in length additional all-round white lights between the lights prescribed in sub-paragraphs (i) and (ii) so that the distance between the lights shall not exceed 100 metres;
(iv) a diamond shape at or near the aftermost extremity of the last vessel or object being towed and if the length of the tow exceeds 200 metres an additional diamond shape where it can best be seen and located as far forward as is practicable.
(h) Where from any sufficient cause it is impracticable for a vessel or object being towed to exhibit the lights or shapes prescribed in paragraph (e) or (g) of this Rule, all possible measures shall be taken to light the vessel or object towed or at least to indicate the presence of such vessel or object.
(i) Where from any sufficient cause it is impracticable for a vessel not normally engaged in towing operations to display the lights prescribed in paragraph (a) or (c) of this Rule, such vessel shall not be required to exhibit those lights when engaged in towing another vessel in distress or otherwise in need of assistance. All possible measures shall be taken to indicate the nature of the relationship between the towing vessel and the vessel being towed as authorised by Rule 36, in particular by illuminating the towline.

44

RULE 25 SAILING VESSELS UNDERWAY AND VESSELS UNDER OARS

(a) A sailing vessel underway shall exhibit:
(i) sidelights;
(ii) sternlights.

(b) In a sailing vessel of less than 20 metres in length the lights prescribed in paragraph (a) of this Rule may be combined in one lantern carried at or near the top of the mast where it can best be seen.

(c) A sailing vessel underway may, in addition to the lights prescribed in paragraph (a) of this Rule, exhibit at or near the top of the mast, where they can best be seen, two all-round lights in a vertical line, the upper being red and the lower green, but these lights shall not be exhibited in conjunction with the combined lantern permitted by paragraph (b) of this Rule.

(d) (i) A sailing vesel of less than 7 metres in length shall, if practicable, exhibit the lights prescribed in paragraph (a) or (b) of this Rule, but if she does not, she shall have ready at hand an electric torch or lighted lantern showing a white light which shall be exhibited in sufficient time to prevent collision.
(ii) A vessel under oars may exhibit the lights prescribed in this Rule for sailing vessels, but if she does not, she shall have ready at hand an electric torch or lighted lantern showing a white light which shall be exhibited in sufficient time to prevent collision.

(e) A vessel proceeding under sail when also being propelled by machinery shall exhibit forward where it can best be seen a conical shape, apex downwards.

RULE 26 FISHING VESSELS

(a) A vessel engaged in fishing, whether underway or at anchor, shall exhibit only the lights and shapes prescribed in this Rule.

(b) A vessel when engaged in trawling, by which is meant the dragging through the water of a dredge net or other apparatus used as a fishing appliance, shall exhibit:
(i) two all-round lights in a vertical line, the upper being green and the other white, or a shape consisting of two cones with their apexes together in a vertical line one above the other:
(ii) a masthead light abaft of and higher than the all-round green light; a vessel of less than 50 metres in length shall not be obliged to exhibit such a light but may do so;
(iii) when making way through the water, in addition to the lights prescribed in this paragraph, sidelights and a sternlight.

(c) A vessel engaged in fishing, other than trawling, shall exhibit:
(i) two all-round lights in a vertical line, the upper being red and the lower white, or a shape consisting of two cones with apexes together in a line one above the other.
(ii) when there is outlying gear extending more than 150 metres horizontally from the vessel, an all-round white light or a cone apex upwards in the direction of the gear;
(iii) when making way through the water, in addition to the lights prescribed in this paragraph, sidelights and a sternlight.

(d) The additional signals described in Annex ii to these Regulations apply to vessels fishing in close proximity to other vessels fishing.

(e) A vessel when not engaged in fishing shall not exhibit the lights or shapes prescribed in thisRule, but only those prescribed for a vessel of her length

RULE 27 VESSELS NOT UNDER COMMAND OR RESTRICTED IN THEIR ABILITY TO MANOEUVRE

(a) A vessel not under command shall exhibit:
(i) two all-round red lights in a vertical line where they can best be seen;
(ii) two balls or similar shapes in a vertical line where they can best be seen;
(iii) when making way through the water, in addition to the lights prescribed in this paragraph, sidelights and a stemlight.

(b) A vessel restricted in her ability to manoeuvre, except a vessel engaged in mine-clearance operations, shall exhibit:
(i) three all-round lights in a vertical line where they can best be seen. The highest and lowest of these lights shall be red and the middle light shall be white;
(ii) three shapes in a vertical line where they can best be seen.The highest and lowest of these shapes shall be balls and the middle one a diamond;
(iii) when making way through the water, a masthead light or lights, sidelights and a sternlight, in additon to the lights prescribed in sub-paragraph (i);
(iv) when at anchor, in addition to the lights or shapes prescribed in sub-paragraphs (i) and (ii), the light, lights or shape prescribed in Rule 30.

(c) A power-driven vessel engaged in a towing operation such as severely restricts the towing vessel and her tow in their ability to deviate from their course shall, in addition to the lights or shapes prescribed in Rule 24(a), exhibit the lights or shapes prescribed in sub-paragraphs (b)(i) and (ii) of this Rule.

(d) A vessel engaged in dredging or underwater operations, when restricted in her ability to manoeuvre, shall exhibit the lights and shapes prescribed in sub-paragraph (b)(ii) and (iii) of this Rule and shall, in addition, when an obstruction exists, exhibit:
(i) two all-round red lights or two balls in a vertical line to indicate the side on which the obstruction exists;
(ii) two all-round green lights or two diamonds in a vertical line to indicate the side on which another vessel may pass;
(iii) when at anchor, the lights or shapes prescribed in this paragraph instead of the lights or shape prescribed in Rule 30.

(e) Whenever the size of a vessel engaged in diving operations makes it impracticable to exhibit all lights and shapes prescribed in paragraph (d) of this Rule, the following shall be exhibited:
(i) three all-round lights in a vertical line where they can best be seen. The highest and lowest of these lights shall be red and the middle light shall be white;
(ii) a rigid replica of the International Code flag "A" not less than 1 metre in height. Measures shall be taken to ensure its all-round visibility.

(f) A vessel engaged in mine-clearance operations shall in addition to the lights prescribed for a power-driven vessel in Rule 23 or to the lights or shape prescribed for a vessel at anchor in Rule 30 as appropriate, exhibit three all-round green lights or three balls. One of these lights or shapes shall be exhibited near the foremast head and one at each end of the fore yard. These lights or shapes indicate that it is dangerous for another vessel to approach within 1000 metres of the mine-clearance vessel.

(g) Vessels of less than 12 metres in length, except those engaged in diving operations, shall not be required to exhibit the lights and shapes prescribed in this Rule.

(h) The signals prescribed in this Rule are not signals of vessels in distress and requiring assistance.

45

RULE 28 VESSELS CONSTRAINED BY THEIR DRAUGHT

A vessel constrained by her draught may, in addition to the lights prescribed for power-driven vessels in Rule 23, exhibit where they can best be seen three all-round red lights in a vertical line, or a cylinder.

RULE 29 PILOT VESSELS

(a) A vessel engaged on pilotage duty shall exhibit:
(i) at or near the masthead, two all-round lights in a vertical line, the upper being white and the lower red;
(ii) when underway, in addition, sidelights and a sternlight;
(iii) when at anchor, in addition to the lights prescribed in sub-paragraph (i), the lights or shape prescribed in Rule 30 for vessels at anchor.
(b) A pilot vessel when not engaged on pilotage duty shall exhibit the lights or shapes prescribed for a similar vessel of her length.

RULE 30 ANCHORED VESSELS AND VESSELS AGROUND

(a) A vessel at anchor shall exhibit where it can best be seen:
(i) in the fore part, an all-round white light or one ball;
(ii) at or near the stern and at a lower level than the light prescribed in sub-paragraph (i), an all-round white light.
(b) A vessel of less than 50 metres in length may exhibit an all-round white light where it can best be seen instead of the lights prescribed in paragraph (a) of this Rule.
(c) A vessel at anchor may, and a vessel of 100 metres and more in length shall, also use the available working or equivalent lights to illuminate her decks.
(d) A vessel aground shall exhibit the lights prescribed in paragraph (a) or (b) of this Rule and in addition, where they can best be seen:
(i) two all-round red lights in a vertical line;
(ii) three balls in a vertical line.
(e) A vessel of less than 7 metres in length, when at anchor not in or near a narrow channel, fairway or anchorage, or where other vessels normally navigate, shall not be required to exhibit the lights or shape prescribed in paragraphs(a) and (b) of this Rule.
(f) A vessel of less than 12 metres in length, when aground, shall not be required to exhibit the lights or shapes prescribed in sub-paragraphs (d)(i) and (ii) of this Rule.

RULE 31 SEAPLANES

Where it is impracticable for a seaplane to exhibit lights and shapes of the characteristics or in the positions prescribed in the Rules of this Part she shall exhibit lights and shapes as closely similar in characteristics and position as is possible.

PART D. SOUND & LIGHT SIGNALS

RULE 32 DEFINITIONS

(a) The word "whistle" means any sound signalling appliance capable of producing the prescribed blasts and which complies with the specifications in Annex III to these Regulations.
(b) The term "short blast" means a blast of about one second's duration.
(c) The term "prolonged blast" means a blast of from four to six seconds' duration.

RULE 33 EQUIPMENT FOR SOUND SIGNALS

(a) A Vessel of 12 metres or more in length shall be provided with a whistle and a bell and a vessel of 100 metres or more in length shall, in addition, be provided with a gong, the tone and sound of which cannot be confused with that of the bell. The whistle, bell and gong shall comply with the specifications in Annex III to these Regulations (not reproduced here). The bell or gong or both may be replaced by other equipment having the same respective sound characteristics, provided that manual sounding of the prescribed signals shall always be possible.
(b) A vessel of less than 12 metres in length shall not be obliged to carry the sound signalling appliances prescribed in paragraph (a) of this Rule but if she does not, she shall be provided with some other means of making an efficient sound signal.

RULE 34 MANOEUVERING AND WARNING SIGNALS

(a) When vessels are in sight of one another, a power-driven vessel underway, when manoeuvering as authorised or required by these Rules, shall indicate that manoeuvre by the following signals on her whistle:
– one short blast to mean
    "I am altering my course to starboard";
– two short blasts to mean
    "I am altering my course to port";
– three short blasts to mean
    "I am operating astern propulsion".
(b) Any vessel may supplement the whistle signals prescribed in paragraph (a) of this Rule by light signals, repeated as appropriate, whilst the manoeuvre is being carried out:
(i) these light signals shall have the following significance:
– one flash to mean
    "I am altering my course to starboard";
– two flashes to mean
    "I am altering my course to port";
– Three flashes to mean
    "I am operating astern propulsion";
(ii) the duration of each flash shall be about one second, the interval between flashes shall be about one second, and at intervals of the successive signals shall be not less than ten seconds;
(iii) the light used for this signal shall, if fitted, be an all-round while light, visible at a minimum range of 5 miles, and shall comply with the provisions of Annex I to these Regulations (not reproduced here).
(c) When in sight of one another in a narrow channel or fairway:
(i) a vessel intending to overtake another shall in compliance with Rule 9 (e)(i) indicate her intention by the following signals on her whistle:
– two prolonged blasts followed by one short blast to mean
    "I intend to overtake you on your starboard side";
– two prolonged blasts followed by two short blasts to mean
    "I intend to overtake you on your port side".
(ii) A vessel about to be overtaken when acting in accordance with Rule 9(e)(i) shall indicate her agreement by the following signal on her whistle:
– one prolonged, one short, one prolonged and one short blast in that order.
(d) When vessels in sight of one another are approaching each other and from any cause either vessel fails to understand the intentions or actions of the other, or is in doubt

whether sufficient action is being taken by the other to avoid collision, the vessel in doubt shall immediately indicate such doubt by giving at least five short and rapid blasts on the whistle. Such signal may be supplemented by a light signal of at least five short and rapid flashes.

(e) A vessel nearing a bend or an area of a channel or fairway where other vessels may be obscured by an intervening obstruction shall sound one prolonged blast. Such signal shall be answered with a prolonged blast by by any approaching vessel that may be within hearing around the bend or behind the intervening obstruction.

(f) If whistles are fitted on a vessel at a distance apart of more than 100 metres, one whistle only shall be used for giving manoeuvring and warning signals.

RULE 35 SOUND SIGNALS IN RESTRICTED VISIBILITY

In or near an area of restricted visibility, whether by day or night, the signals prescribed in this Rule shall be used as follows:

(a) A power-driven vessel making way through the water shall sound at intervals of not more than 2 minutes one prolonged blast.

(b) A power-driven vessel underway but stopped and making no way through the water shall sound at intervals of not more than 2 minutes two prolonged blasts in succession with an intervals of about 2 seconds between them.

(c) A vessel not under command, a vessel restricted in her ability to manoeuvre, a vessel constrained by her draft, a sailing vessel, a vessel engaged in fishing and a vessel engaged in towing or pushing another vessel shall, instead of the signals prescribed in paragraphs (a) or (b) of this Rule, sound at intervals of not more than 2 minutes three blasts in succession, namely one prolonged followed by two short blasts.

(d) A vessel engaged in fishing, when at anchor, and a vessel restricted in her ability to manoeuvre when carrying out her work at anchor, 'shall instead of the signals prescribed in paragraph (g) of this Rule sound the signal prescribed in paragraph (c) of this Rule.

(e) A vessel towed or if more than one vessel is towed the last vessel of the tow, if manned, shall at intervals of not more than 2 minutes sound four blasts in succession, namely one prolonged followed by three short blasts. When practicable, this signal shall be made immediately after the signal made by the towing vessel.

(f) When a pushing vessel and a vessel being pushed ahead are rigidly connected in a composite unit they shall be regarded as a power-driven vessel and shall give the signals prescribed in paragraphs (a) or (b) of this Rule.

(g) A vessel at anchor shall at intervals of not more than one minute ring the bell rapidly for about 5 seconds. In a vessel of 100 metres or more in length the bell shall be sounded in the forepart of the vessel and immediately after the ringing of the bell the gong shall be sounded rapidly for about 5 seconds in the after part of the vessel. A vessel at anchor may in addition sound three blasts in succession, namely one short, one prolonged and one short blast, to give warning of her position and of the possibility of collision to an approaching vessel.

(h) A vessel aground shall give the bell signal and if required the gong signal prescribed in paragraph (g) of this Rule and shall, in addition, give three separate and distinct strokes on the bell immediately before and after the rapid ringing of the bell. A vessel aground may in addition sound an appropriate whistle signal.

(i) A vessel of less than 12 metres in length shall not be obliged to give the above-mentioned signals but, if she does not, shall make some other efficient sound signal at intervals of not more than 2 minutes.

(j) A pilot vessel when engaged on pilotage duty may in addition to the signals prescribed in paragraphs (a), (b) or (g) of this Rule sound an identity signal consisting of four short blasts.

RULE 36 SIGNALS TO ATTRACT ATTENTION

If necessary to attract the attention of another vessel any vessel may make light or sound signals that cannot be mistaken for any signal authorised elsewhere in these Rules, or may direct the beam of her searchlight in the direction of the danger, in such a way as not to embarrass any vessel. Any light to attract the attention of another vessel shall be such that it cannot be mistaken for any aid to navigation. For the purpose of this Rule the use of high intensity intermittent or revolving lights, such as strobe lights, shall be avoided.

RULE 37 DISTRESS SIGNALS

When a vessel is in distress and requires assistance she shall use or exhibit the signals described in Annex IV to these Regulations.

DISTRESS SIGNALS

1. The following signals used or exhibited, either together or separately, indicate distress and need of assistance.

(a) a gun or explosive signal fired at intervals of about a minute
(b) a continuous sounding with any fog-signalling apparatus
(c) rockets or shells throwing red stars
(d) SOS in the morse code by R/T or any other signalling method
(e) the spoken word MAYDAY sent by R/T
(f) the International Code Distress Signal NC
(g) a signal consisting of a square flag and a ball
(h) flames on the vessel
(i) a red rocket flare or red hand flare
(j) an orange smoke signal
(k) slowly and repeatedly raising and lowering arms outstretched on each side
(l) (m) the radiotelegraph and radiotelephone alarm signals
(n) signals transmitted by emergency position-indicating radio beacons (EPIRBs)
(o) approved signals transmitted by telecommunication systems
(p) the digital selective calling distress signals

It is forbidden to use any of these signals except as a sign of distress and needing assistance.

Clearly some of these distress signals are unsuitable for use by small craft. A MAYDAY message made by VHF is likely to be the most commonly used method of asking for assistance. But flares are also still important, especially for small craft not carrying a VHF radio. Red hand flares can be useful to pinpoint the vessel's position for approaching rescue craft.

> **A mariner not only has to know how to make a distress signal if it becomes necessary, but he must also be able to recognize distress signals made by others. This could include dinghies, sailboards, and even those stranded on the beach.**